SPINACH SAVES THE DAY

Beginners Guide to Writing Children's Books

G. P. Jontz, Anthropoligist

Illustrations by Franklin T. Straw

ABOUT THE AUTHOR: G.P. Jontz, Anthropologist, resides in Indianapolis, Indiana

Dedicated to Swan and Jerry my sons who always inspire and motivate me to do my best regardless of how difficult things get at times. Thanks so much for always being there and may this book inspire you both to never give up your dreams!

Copyright © 2014 by PSI/HGP PUBLISHING
All rights reserved.
ISBN-10:0988243636
ISBN-13:978-0-9882436-3-7

Lesson 1: Dream, Outline & Write

Combining Work and Pleasure

Like every doctor lawyer or Indian chief, a writer must curtail their creativity to meet the demands of their reality and we can only hope to achieve a balance between the two.

In the case of "SPINACH SAVES THE DAY! . . ." as with "SEEDS OF ADAM . . ." my need to earn a living forces me to publish a rough draft of this work in progress. In so doing, I encourage any beginning writer of adult or children's literature to literally outline your dreams the moment you have them and get to a pen and paper as quickly as possible. This way when reality comes to awaken you from your dreams they are somewhat documented in order to come back to them later.

As with "SEEDS OF ADAM . . .", "SPINACH SAVES THE DAY . . ." will definitely have a sequel and possibly be made into a movie at some date. It is with that hope and spirit that I encourage all beginning writers to buy this book and follow along the path to successfully write books that will provide a lifetime of enjoyment to people of all ages while providing a fun way to learn how to deal effectively with difficult but necessary evils we all face at one time or another.

Many humble thanks to those of you who purchase this book for your young ones or as a tool to learn some of the bitter sweet lessons that life tends to be merciless in teaching us.

Godspeed prosperity, love and happiness,

G.P. Jontz

SPINACH SAVES THE DAY

Beginners Guide to Writing Children's Books

G. P. Jontz, Anthropoligist

Illustrations by Franklin T. Straw

CHAPTER ONE

A STAND THAT ENDS IN BED

'Twas a cold and starry Spring night after dinner when a young boy named Quique was sent to bed early for not eating his green salad because he hated green vegetables. It wasn't the first time nor would it be the last for Quique vowed that night to never eat anything green again and meant it. "I'm never going to eat green vegetables, especially not spinach." he said sticking out his toung in disgust and frowning at the thought of taking one bite of the most detestable green yucky stuff he'd ever known. "I hate spinach!" he said.

"Then off to bed with you young man. You shant have desert if you cant eat your spinach!" said his Mom while removing the fork with a big piece of chocolate cake on it that he was about to shovel into his mouth.

"Mom! No, that's not fair." cried Quique looking at his Grandpa for sympathy.

"You heard me. Now off to bed." Said his Mom and Quique angrily scuffed off to bed.

"Why on earth would you say a thing like that boy? My Grandma always told me spinach saved the day. I sure do miss my Grandma now that she's entered the happy hunting grounds where all our ancestors live." said his Grandfather standing in the doorway of Quique's room with his crikety wooden rocking chair. Grandpa hadn't spoken a word in weeks. He'd mostly just sit at the dinner table and eat very little even when Quique's Mom scolded him and Quique about not eating enough after she'd stood over a hot stove cooking for them. Grandpa would just sit in his rocking chair staring out the window at the trees mostly.

That night Grandpa pulled his favorite rocking chair beside his grandson Quique's small bed, then he sat in it and began rocking to and fro and chanting an old Indian burial song. I guess Grandpa really did miss his Grandma because he said the chanting would summons her back to tell the story of how spinach saved the day. It sounded like a crazy idea to Quique, but he loved his Grandpa's stories and was glad to have the company after missing out on his favorite desert for making what he felt was a reasonable objection.

The rhythmic chant and constant beat of the wooden rocker hitting against the hardwood floor sounded a bit like drums and wind blowing through the room to Young Quique. His Grandpa often sang Indian songs that he'd learned as a child but never a chant that was meant to summons Quique's Great Great Grandma, Cleopatra Quique, said to be a Blackfeet Indian Princess and leader of a tribe of Blackfeet Indians that lived long long ago.

After listening to his Grandpa's thumping and chanting for what felt like a very long time, Quique was having a hard time staying awake. "She must be very busy. . ." thought Quique ". . .because she hasn't come to see Grandpa yet." Quique rubbed his eyes as the rhythm of the beating drums and chant began to make him sleepy.

"Huh, uohway huh! Huh uohway huh! Yawway huh! Yaway huh huh huh!" chanted Grandpa Quique. "What does that mean Grandpa?" Quique asked.

CHAPTER TWO

THE CHANT

"This is the chant to summon your ancestors from the Blackfeet Indian Tribe where your Great-Great Grandmother Cleopatra was Chieftain of Dragonia, the land known as the Realm of Dragons and Giants." said Grandpa. He continued his chanting and rocking until soon his sleepy eyed Grandson forgot all about being sent to bed early for not eating his green vegetable salad and vowing to always hate spinach.

As Quique slumbered he dreamt of voices from afar that came from way down deep and under the mossy bogs of the Blackfeet Indian burial grounds, where whispering winds and swirling leaves spun a tale of a battle fought oh so long ago.

It was as if Quique could hear the voice of his Blackfeet Indian ancestor, his Great -Great Grandma, Chieftain Cleopatra Quique, guardian of Vipers and Vegemites saying:

"Yes, there was a time when giants and dragons roamed the mossy bogs and trees could walk and talk as men, for all things did have life amongst the mystic creatures when Spinach saved the day."

After listening to his Grandpa's chant, Young Quique seemed to wake up in an enchanted garden. He sat up in his bed and rubbed his sleepy eyes. He somehow knew this had to be the place his Grandpa had spoken of. It was the place where our Blackfeet ancestors had lived many moons ago as Grandpa often put it.

His Grandpa had finally summoned his Great-Great Grandma, Chieftain Cleopatra and Quique was now floating upward towards a billowing cloud where the Indian Princess, Chieftain Cleopatra sat Indian style watching over Dragonia, the land she ruled known as home of Dragons and Giants. Quique never suspected the tales his Grandpa always told him about his Blackfeet Indian ancestors were true until

now for what appeard before his eyes was nothing short of a miracle.

Quique believed his Grandpa's chanting must have made him float high above his bed right into the Indian Burial Ground he'd told him about as the chant grew fainter and further away. Then he heard the Princess Chieftain softly call his name. He continued floating upward towards her voice until he could no longer hear his grandfather's chanting or the constant beating of the rocking chair.

CHAPTER THREE

THE PRINCESS CHIEFTAN

When Quique was close enough to see her, it was if she were peering into his heart searching for answers to questions he didn't even know he had. Quique didn't know what he should ask or say to the Great Princess Chieftain. Then he remembered his Grandpa saying she once told him something about spinach saving the day and decided he would ask her what she meant when she told his Grandpa about that. "How can spinach save the day?" asked Quique.

"Your question is very wise Young Quique so I will now try to answer it with the wisdom it deserves. As the story goes . . ." began Quique's Great-Great Grandma, Chieftain Cleopatra and the curiosity in Quique's earthly brown and green eyes glistened like a waking forest glistens from morning dew. As with every growing leaf and blade of grass that are quenched with each droplet of dew, Quique's thirst for knowledge and adventure were quenched with anticipation of hearing the greatest story ever told.

He felt like a bird in the sky that was capable of seeing all things because he too was peering through a cloud where his ancestor sat perched like a great eagle. Quique could barely hear it but his Grampa's chanting and the faint drum beat were still in the background and he felt a cool breeze brush against his cheek.

What began as a time out in his bedroom was now the adventure of a life time as the sound of his Grandpa's rocking and chanting seemed to lead him somewhere he'd never seen before.

"What's that boy?" Grandpa asked, interrupting his chanting and rocking as he noticed that Young Quique was mumbling something even though it appeared he had fallen asleep. "Did I hear you say you'd like to know how Spinach could save the day?" Grandpa said leaning closer to hear a question his Grandson muttered in his sleep.

"What a strange thing to ask." thought Quique's Grandpa as he patted the boy on the head and tucked the blanket snuggly around his sleeping Grandson then resumed rocking and chanting.

Little did Grandpa know that his chant to summon his Grandma, the Princess Chieftain Cleopatra had actually worked!

CHAPTER FOUR

JOURNEY TO VEGEMITE VILLAGE

Suddenly Grandpa stopped rocking and chanting. He reared back in his rocking chair where he sat next to Quique's tiny bed and looked up at the ceiling in deep recollection, scratching his head and said:

"...Hmm, I do recall what my Grandmother said now...

"It was said that Squire Spinach Green Leaf was quite a rambunctious lad that often imagined he might slay dragons and giants someday to rescue his Lady Roma Tomato, whom Spinach would imagine was a beautiful princess in distress. She said he would spend hours on end in the garden swinging his pretend sword chasing away imaginary dragons and giants."

As Young Quique listened, he was still floating high above the Village where magical creatures lived as he listened to his Great Great Grandma Chieftain Cleopatra explain how Spinach could save the day.

"So there weren't really any dragons or giants then, only pretend ones?" asked Quique rubbing his eyes not knowing whether he was still asleep or not.

"I didn't say there weren't any real dragons and giants; Squire Spinach had heard about them but he'd never met any real ones until much later." said the Chieftain.

"Oh, please tell me how he meets the real ones! I would really like to hear about the dragons and giants and magical creatures". said Quique bouncing up and down on the cloud where he sat with his legs crossed Indian style.

"Alright I will tell you where you must go to find a map that will lead you to them." said the lovely Princess Chieftain.

"A map?" asked Quique

"Yes. The map hidden in the Mossy Bogland of the Indian Burial Ground. When you find the map you'll be able to find Dragonia and visit the Giants and Dragons that lived there for yourself." said the Chieftain.

CHAPTER FIVE

ACTIVITIES FOR EXPLOERS

Can you find the map? If you find it, circle the map of the Mossy Boglands.

Look at the map of the Indian Burial Grounds and draw a circle around the Burial Ground.

Take a closer look at a real Indian Burial Ground.

You have found the Indian Burial Grounds. See how the Indian Burial Grounds look close up and keep your eyes open for giants and dragons that protect these realms. At one time giant nomadic Indians planted all sorts of seed in Vegemite Village, but they didn't grow fast enough for them to escape the deadliest winter of all times. The nomadic Indian tribe had to leave for a warmer climate to survive and leave all their belongings to make traveling to their new home easier on them. They left everything behind including all the seedlings they planted and the fertilizer they used to grow their gardens and had to rebuild with nothing but what they found along the way so many of them died before their plants or children could grow.

CHAPTER FIVE

THE ROOT OF THE PROBLEM

One day a miraculous discovery was made by the insects and seedlings left behind that helped them become so much stronger and smarter that they began to care for themselves. Their discovery became buried into the valley once inhabited by the nomads for centuries until things that once were thought to be inanimate began walking and talking as part of their daily lives.

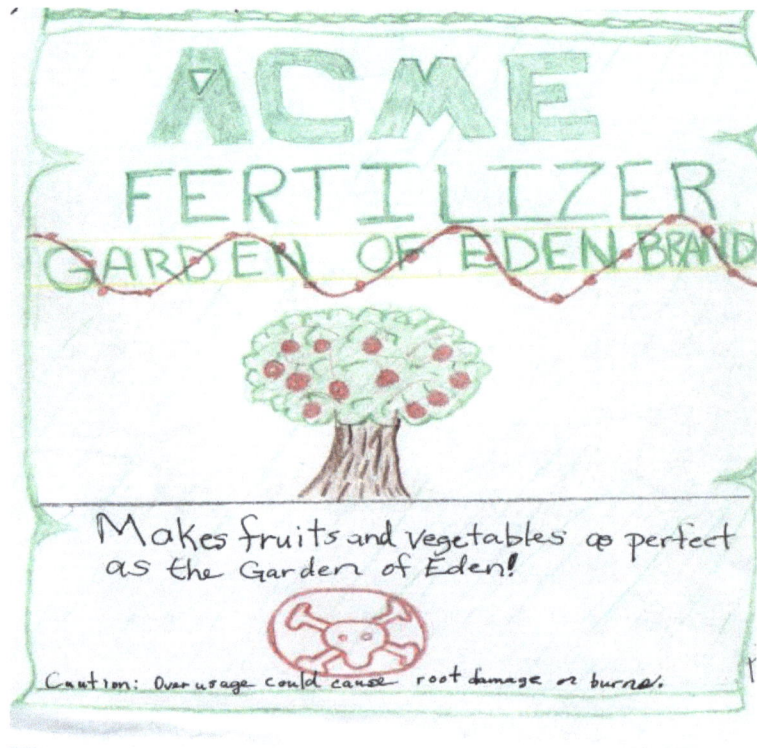

CHAPTER SIX

BEAUTY'S ONLY SKIN DEEP

Many years later Vegemite Village was formed and the Vegimite Councl uncovered a special tonic that would make them perfect. More perfect than ever before known.

"You'll be the envy of all". Councilman Corn postured.

"Do you think it will make the ladies like me more?" said Councilman Onion.

"I doubt that." Said Mrs. Tomatoe, but my daughter , Roma, will just love it. Then again she and Clemintine were winners in the Easter Egg pagent three times in a row. You don't get much more perfect than that." Boasted Mrs. Tomatoe.

The Council sought out volunteers to test the tonic on and found more than enough eager Vegimites.

There was one Vegemite in the far end of the Garden who wasn't so eager.

Mr. Egg Plant didn't much care for company but couldn't help overhearing all the fuss about some new Acne Beauty Tonic.

"No thank you. I don't want any of that stuff and I hope they don't come over here pestering me about being a volunteer." thought Mr. Egg Plant. He never understood why he'd lost the last few Easter Egg Pageants he'd entered when his skin was a perfect color purple and smoother than an Easter Egg.

Instead of becoming better though the beautiful fruits and vegies didn't feel very well after trying the special tonic given to them by the Vegemite Counsel. Their roots and gardens began to appear burned all around.

Then a little crab apple told a big lie. "It was the dragons and giants!" said the little crab-apple to get attention. He was tired of having to take second place to the bigger apples at the pageant and decided be first with important news for a change.

"I saw Brussle and Spinach when they went there!" said Crab Apple. "Now everyone will look up to me." he thought after telling the lie that made most of the Vegimites that heard him start to panic from fear of an attack by the giants and dragons.

But the very tall Mrs. Sun Flower, who was a previous winner of the padgent turned judge just kept right on smiling because she had seen more than most of the Vegemites, being that she was the tallest and most privy to any news in the Village, yet she hadn't seen any dragons.

"Oh dear, what about the padgent? I was a shoe in this year." Said Crafty Carrot.

"They must have stired up the dragons and giants. They're the ones responsible for the burned gardens all around the village and now we have to cancel the padgent." Said Mr. Tomatoe worried about his nephew Brussle Sprout who was always thought of as the "green tomatoe" of the family tree.

"Brussle, you really got the short end of the stick. You inherited your family's roundness but your complexion is that horrible green color. No wonder you like hanging arund with Spinach." teased the Hot Pepper Gang after hearing about the trouble Brussle and Spinach were in. "Now you've got the whole Village after you!" the young village vegies said.

"Brainiac Brocoli of the Vegemite Intelligence Agency will have to go undercover to investigate what the Lettuce and Spinace Counsel are up to in this matter about the dragons and giants. I suspect they may be trying to use them as a weapon of sorts" said Mr. Tomatoe. ". . .and keep this between us will you. I don't want to alert Mrs Tomatoe or the full Counsel until I get to the bottom of this" he said to Brocoli.

After being teased to tears by the Hot Peper Gang and the young vegies, Brussle ran off by himself.

"Ill show them!" he said. Then he sat off in the direction of where he'd heard many say they had seen Squire Spinach fighting with dragons and giants. He too wanted to learn to fight dragons so he wouldn't be teased so much about his size and color. He stopped to fashion a sword out of a branch he'd found lying on the ground then continued on his way to find Squire Spinach until he ran into his cousin Clementine. She was a pesty little fruitcake that he would have just as soon not ever have to speak with especially not now. "What do you want Clemintine?" he asked sounding annoyed.

"Oh boy, you're in big trouble now Brussle!" she said.
"Nuh uh, shut up Clementine! He replied even more annoyed by her tone of voice than he was at the Hot Pepper Gang who made him want to prove his bravery and worth by slaying dragons in the first place. He looked at his weapon and decided he would practice using it on Clemtine if she said one more word to get on his nerves.
"I saw you up on the Hilltop with that weirdo Spinach Leaf that's always talking to himself and I'm going to tell this time if you head back there again." She said trying to act like she was a grown up orange instead of just the little fruit that she was.
"You're a liar!" Brussle yelled at her lifting his sword and pointing it at her. "I should run you through for telling lies on me." he said.
"Bring it!" she said. Clemintine picked up a pointed stick and held it out like she was ready to sword fight with Brussle.
Were it not for her cousin Roma stepping in to break up there fight, the two would have had at it!

"Alright you two that's enough." Said Roma

"He's been going to see that weirdo Spinach everyone's been talking about." Clemintine told Roma.

"Well, it sounds like he's not the only one who's in trouble. If you know so much about it, you must have been there too!" said Roma.

"Oh you just like that green weirdo Spinach because he always calls you his Lady Roma." Said Clemintine smirking.

"I'm warning you Clem!" Roma said giving Clemintine a look that could kill. "Now you BOTH better play nice or else you're BOTH going to be in trouble if you don't stop fighting." said Roma emphasizing the word both.

"That's my sweet tomatoe! A chip off the old vine." Said Mr. Tomatoe who'd just come home from the Vegemite Counsel. "You kids listen to Roma and you'll stay out of trouble." He said.

"She just likes that Green boy because he's always talking about how he's going to save his Lady Roma from the big bad dragons and giants!" said Clemintine.

"Alright there's to be no more talk about dragons and giants today is that clear young one?" said Mr. Tomatoe. "I'm still trying to figure out how they could have burned the village before the Counsel is in session and your cousin Brussle's going to need all the support he can get as it is!." Then he noticed Brussle and Peafly as they taking off in the direction of the Spinach Patch.

CHAPTER SEVEN

THE CHASE

Brussle had encountered Peafly, an old friend he'd not seen in a while who said he'd let him ride on his back to see the Village from high up in the sky once and now he needed his help to clear his name. "Peafly, will you fly me over to the Lettuce and Spinach Patch?" asked Brussle. Peafly anxious to see an old friend landed next to Brussle and then lowered his head for him to climb on and they were off to the Spinach and Lettuce Patch just in time before Brussle's Uncle Tomatoe had come home or he wouldn't have been allowed to go to the reclusive Spinach and Lettuce Patch.

"Glad to help you my friend. I was just headed that way to visit some distant relatives." buzzed Peafly to Brussle. Then he lifted off the ground with Brussle on his back to journey into the Lettuce and Spinach Patch and seek out Squire Spinach. Brainiac Brocoli spotted them and followed on foot disguised as a green bush because he was unlikely to be noticed that way. With his bushy green head he'd fit right in with the other green vegetation and bushes allowed in those parts.

They soon arrived in the land of lettuce and spinach patches. Peafly flew lower and lower until Brussle could be heard from above the gardens of that area like a big booming alarm.

"Where is Squire Spinach?" shouted Brussle hovering high above a brigade of insects gathering around them on the ground.

From the view of Peafly's back the Lettuce and Spinach Patch , the Onion Patch and all of the reclusive Vegemites could be seen as clear as day. However, as they got closer to the Lettuce and Spinach Counsel they were greeted by the Armed Insect Guard of that Realm.

When Brussle jumped down off Peafly's back, the insects surrounded him. Brussle was halted by a Captain June bug and his line of soldier ants shouting "Cease his weapon!" The ants took the sword Brussle had made and handed it to Captain June Bug. They then allowed him to approach the Captain.

"You are a long way from the village cabage patch Little Sprout! State your business here before I make coleslaw out of you boy." Captain June Bug said with a southern drawl."

Peafly was still hovering high above the colony of Soldier Ants and Captain June Bug. He couldn't land though because the colony of soldier ants threatened to bite Peafly if he tryied to land for allowing Brussle Sprout to jump off his back into their territory. "No one may enter these lands without our permission or the consent of the Lettuce and Spinach Council." They shouted at Peafly hovering above them.

"See hear young Sprout . . ." began Captain June Bug climbing onto a tree stump and looking at Brussle Sprout condescendingly. ". . .the ants and June Bugs have a long standing relationship with the Spinach and Lettuce Council of Elders that dates back to when they were tiny seedlings." While Captain June Bug stood there wearing his red and black coat of honor, he looked like one of the old noble June Bugs about to give a speech on the tree stump where his forefathers had once stood and gave the same speech that he was about to give Brussle.

"The green leaf seedlings were once abandoned by a nomad Indian tribe that promised to care for them. The crops of lettuce and spinach seeds nearly died from neglect until our Forefather June Bugs found them and nursed them back to health. In return they gave those June Bugs and other insects in these lands exclusive rights to see that no harm ever again befell upon them in exchange for food and shelter provided by their lovely green leaves as they matured. As long as the green leaflings do not wonder outside of this realm June Bugs and other insects may consider this the land of plenty and home of the brave. That is why everyone far and near respects our reclusive lifestyle and no one comes in or out without our permission. "

Brussle swallowed hard when he saw the Captain slam his sword into the stump to emphasize his words. Then Brussle noticed out of the corner of his eye that something green and busy was slithering by them on the ground as the Captain continued his speech.

"Now, do you understand that you and that flying contraption that dropped you off here are in violation of our most sacred tradidtion and that it is my responsibility to decide what to do about that violation boy!" he said pointting the tiny sword he'd apprehended from Brussle at him as though he wanted to slice Brussle in half.

"But Captain sir, I must speak to Squire Spinach because he and I have been accused of causing the Dragons to attack our village." Pleaded Brussle.

"I highly doubt that could be true boy; however, some of the younger leaflings have been known to break with tradition from time to time. Did I hear you say the name of this scoundrel might be Squire Spinach,? I believe he is a known repeat offender of leaving our reclusive garden?" Growled the Captain.

"Yes, said Brussle, he and I were both seen playing near the boarder of Dragonia but the truth is that there we never saw any dragons there. I must speak to Squire Spinach to prove I'm not the one who stired up the dragons." Said Brussle.

In the mean time, while the Captain lectured Brussle, Brocoli reached the Coucil of Elders. The oldest Green leaves of Lettuce and Spinach were astounded when they heard the busy green headed Brocoli who'd slithered right next to their patch ask:

"Where is Squire Spinach!"

The elders said nothing though as they were unaccustomed to answering questions, especially questions coming from a stalk of broccoli or any other vegimites that came from the village below since all of Vegimite Village knew that the Lettuce and Spinach Patch were the most detestable and reclusive vegetables in the land except for Onions, who were so stinky they made everyone cry who came near them unless they too were an onion.

"There he is, there's my uncle Spinach going up the hill to Dragonia" Said Lil Lettuce, Spinach's little sister as she took off running to catch up with her favorite brother Spinach.

"After him!" shouted Captain June Bug as he jumped off of the stump dropping the tiny sword he held.

The Soldier Ants turned and began running towards Spinach in an unorganized frenzy.

At that moment, Peafly saw and took his opportunity to rescue Brussle from his captives and Brussle managed to grab his little sword off the ground just in the nick of time while making his escape.

Brocoli slithered up the hill after Lil Lettuce after hearing her say she saw Squire Spinace. Lil Lettuce pursued her Uncle Spinach up the hill towards Dragonia and Peafly and Brussle followed from above ground. The chase was on.

The hill to Dragonia became very steep which slowed down Captain June Bug and his army enough for Spinach and his little sister to ditch them by hiding behind a big rock between an Onion Patch and a cave where they usually practiced fighting Dragons and Giants.

Captain June Bug and his Army of Ants ran right past Lil Lettuce and Spinach into the cave thinking they surely had them cornered.

"The wouldn't have gone in the direction of the Onion Patch so keep on going this way." Said the Captain to his Army of Soldier Ants. The cave pathways went on for a very long time and only lead them back into the Lettuce and Spinach patch where the chase had first begun. Uncertain whether or not Spinach was ever seen or whether this was another example of how undisciplined the young green leafs had become, the Captain called off the search for Spinach.

"Our prisoners have escaped because of a prank committed by an undisciplined delinquent green leaves! From now on, we will have zero tolerance for this sort of behavior beginning with early shut curfew in the malls for any under aged green leaf caught without special permission from our squad leader or an adult escort!" he said standing on the stump to his Army of Soldier Ants.

"Now, back to your posts!" he said stepping down from the stump

"Attention!" said the Sargeant of Arms Soldier Ant while the Captain walked past the army to the June Bug Quarters.

CHAPTER EIGHT

FEE FIE FOE FRIEND

"At Ease Sargeant." Said the Captain and the soldiers went back to their traditional duty of standing guard of the Lettuce and Spinach Patch.

Peafly and Brussle could see from high above exactly where Squire Spinach had hidden with his little sister Lettuce and that the two of them were playing behind a big rock just before the path that leads to Dragonia.

"There he is talking to himself just like Clemintine and everyone in our village said he does so maybe he is crazy enough to stir up the Dragons and Giants!" said Brussle to Peafly who shook his head in disagreement to what Brussle thought.

Peafly came close enough to see that Brocoli had slithered up the hill and was spying on Spinach and his little sister to gather information for the Vegimite Council as he'd been trained to do by the Vegimite Secret Intelligence Agency. Then Peafly and Brussle saw it was Lil Lettuce that Spinach was speaking with as they played like a big rock was a Dragon and an even bigger tree was a Giant.

"Oh hello!" said Lil Lettuce.

Spinach didn't look surprised to see Brussle and Peafly. "You must not talk to strangers>" Spinach said to Lil Lettuce ignoring Brussle and Peafly.

"But Uncle Spinach, didn't you say I shouldn't believe the only friends Ihave are in the Lettuce and Spinach Patch we live in?" asked Lil Lettuce.

"You're right Lil Lettuce. I did say that; so let's you and I give our new friends a proper greeting." Said Spinach.

"You really don't talk to yourself the way everyone says whose seen you from where we live. You've been talking to that little lettuce leaf!" said Brocoli. He poked his green bushy head up from the ground. Spinach and Lil Lettuce were startled at first then laughed at the sudden appearance of a talking stalk of Brocoli which had quite cleverly concealed itself as a green bush.

"Guess that's why it pays to explore the land." Buzzed Peafly.

They all laughed at Peafly's comment.

"What brings you strangers to the outer edge of the Lettuce and Spinach Patch?" asks Spinach.

"It's been reported by some of the villagers where we live that you, Squire Spinach have been battling giants and dragons on the hilltop in Dragonia which caused them to retaliate against our village by burning it" Brocoli read from a parchment he held in his hand.

"That's not true. I've never been to the hilltop; nor have I ever really seen a giant or a single dragon!" replied Spinach.

"My Uncle Spinach has been showing me how to fight dragons and giants by pretending this big rock is a dragon and that tall tree is a giant." Said Lil Lettuce.

"Would you like to play too then we won't be strangers any more?" she asked her new friends.

Brocoli looked at Brussle and Peafly wondering how the rumor of Spinach and Brussle got started up and said: "Well the news of your innocence will put your Uncle Tomatoe at ease when he hears this, but if you and Spinach didn't stir up the dragons then why did they burn the village? He pondered.

"Just then a voice in the clouds said: "They didn't do it either."

"Who goes there?" said Squire Spinach. He looked towards the cave afraid Captain June Bug and his army had discovered his hideout.

"Who said that?" said Broccoli. Then he switched into his stealth mode appearance of tumbleweed and began rolling around trying to find the voice he heard.

"Look up there!" said Brussle and Lil Spinach pointing at a cloud.

Broccoli stopped rolling around and stood motionless with his eyes looking upward toward where Lil Spinach and Brussle were pointing.

"Up in the sky!" said Spinach now staring at a big cloud that loomed above the Hilltop overlooking where they now stood.

"There's something behind that cloud!" buzzed Peafly.

"Perhaps we should tell your elders about this." said Broccoli to Squire Spinach.

"Why, they'd just sit there and do nothing like they always do." Said Lil Lettuce.

"You're right, Lil Lettuce, we should go and explore this ourselves." Said Spinach.

"We will be able to get a closer look if we go up to the Hilltop." said Peafly.

"Have you ever gone that far away from Vegemite Village Peafly?" asked Brussle.

"Yes, all the time. There's nothing to be afraid of." Peafly said.

So the all started up the Hilltop and were stopped in their tracks at the sight of a boy giant sitting on a cloud.

"Who are you?" said the boy giant to the group of five Vegemites traveling upward to the highest point of the Hilltop.

"I am called Peafly and Brussle Sprout rides atop my back. I have come here many times before to visit my relatives. They are dragons that only come to visit during the solstice moon and what are you called boy giant?

"I am Quique, here in this far away land in search of the land of Dragonia where dragons and giants once dwelled according to my Blackfeet Indiana ancestor. Said Quique.

The others soon made it up to the highest point of the Hilltop where Peafly and Brussle were hovering above beneath a cloud. "Who is that?" said Spinach.

"It is Quique in search of dragons and giants like us." Said Brussle.

"But you are a boy giant so why would you have to search for your own kind?" said Broccoli revealing his true identity was not really a tumbleweed.

"I'm no giant, I'm just a boy, although, I suppose to a talking stalk of Broccoli I may seem a bit larger than you're used to seeing." Said Quique.

"Are the dragons inside the clouds too?" asked Lil Lettuce.

"No, only my Great-great Grandmother, Chieftain Cleopatra Quique of the Blackfoot Indian Tribes that once roamed these lands and now are buried atop that hill in the Indian Burial Grounds.

"But that's where legend has it that giants ad dragons live" said Broccoli. "I take pride in being very knowledgeable about these matters." He boasted then pulled out a picture of a dragon sitting on top of a hill and handed it to Quique, the boy giant. "You see this sacred scroll has been passed down from the time when giants lived among us before they all migrated to this Hilltop. It was said that a great fire followed by freezing rains and snow caused them to leave everything behind when they left their homes and gardens in Vegemite Valley. The seedlings had to grew wild and untamed until the Vegemite Council of Elders brought order so that we could survive and continue to thrive without the giants who once tilled the lands and kept us safe from harm." Broccoli finished his interpretation of the sacred scroll and appeared quite pleased with himself.

Quique looked at the picture and said: "I've seen something just like that before from where I come from. This looks like the back of a book of matches and they can cause . . ." Quique is interrupted before he could finish what he was saying by Broccoli.

"Well, now we can at least be sure it was the dragons that attacked our village. I'm going to have to get back to tell the Council right away." Broccoli said hurrying down the hillside. "I must get there and tell them to prepare for war before the dragons return." Said Broccoli as he returned to his disguise of tumbleweed so not to get caught by Captain June Bugs Army while returning to his own village with this important Intel.

"But there hasn't been any proof that the dragons are responsible. You could be mistaken about them like you were about Squire Spinach and me." Said Brussle.

"Yea!" buzzed Peafly sounding quite agitated.

As Broccoli scurried down from wince he came, Spinach and Lil Lettuce turned and asked Brussle, Peafly and Quique to stay and continue exploring with them to discover whether or not there were any dragons on the Hilltop. Then Quique floated down from the cloud to join them. In their quest to find whether there were any dragons left in the land where the wise Chieftain said the map would lead Quique to see for himself. Quique was happy to have met his strange new friends to keep him company along the way.

After reaching the Hilltop and finding the Indian Burial Ground they made camp and waited until morning to continue searching. While they slept, the sound of the drum beating faintly in the background began and the Chieftain Cleopatra appeared on the cloud once again.

She told Quique that his journey to find the Dragon was the right path and that his new friends would help him to see what needs to be done.

"The dragon you are searching for is like glass and will be very easy to miss if you peer through it impatiently. So rest before going on your quest for the Glass Dragon." Said Chieftain Cleopatra as the faint drumbeat became louder and the chanting of Quique's grandfather sounded in the background.

CHAPTER 9

THE ADVENTURE BEGINS

When Quique awoke, he was in his bed. The smell of toast, grits eggs and bacon cooking on the stove poured into Quique's bedroom. He could hear his mother stirring around in the kitchen and saw his Grandpa had fallen sound asleep in his favorite rocking chair beside his bed that somehow didn't seem so tiny any more after such a wondrous adventure. He looked forward to sharing the next adventure with his Grandpa and thought of his new friends on the way to breakfast and hoped they'd get to meet again in the quest to find the glass dragon but that's another story.

THE END

AUTHOR'S COMMENTS

This children's fairy tale contained notations on some of the pictures to provide one method of keeping track of important characters in the story that may be used at a later.

One of the problems I always seem to encounter is pagination issues that may occur when you have to use different computers that may not use the same programs or software. Compatibility issues that can result from this could cause you to have to manually input your page numbers which is a real bumber but does resolve the problem of switching from say a pdf back to an older version of Microsoft Word for example. Just be sure to save a couple of copies of your book in case an older version causes you to lose pictures or more advanced formatting.

When adding pictures to your book, I found it helps to save all the pictures separately and then copy paste them with your text. Again, make a couple of copies of this with different file names in case of compatibility issues so you don't lose any of your work.

In the next "Spinach Saves The Day!" Series you will get to see more editing techniques and get a hands on feel for what a finished product should look like. Hope this gets you started writing your Children's book and watch for the next issue and different products that can be derived from one children's book.

G.P. Jontz

www.ingramcontent.com/pod-product-compliance
Lightning Source LLC
Chambersburg PA
CBHW041536040426

42446CB00002B/117